The
Queen
of
Wands

The Queen of Wands

Poetry by

JUDY GRAHN

THE CROSSING PRESS / Trumansburg, New York 14886
The Crossing Press Feminist Series

Book and cover design by Mary A. Scott
Cover illustration by Janice Angelini/Penknife Studios
Photograph of Judy Grahn by Wendy Cadden
Typesetting by Martha J. Waters

Printed in the U.S.A.

Library of Congress Cataloging in Publication Data

Grahn, Judy, 1940-
     The queen of wands.

     (The Crossing Press feminist series)
     1. Heroines--Poetry.   I. Title.   II. Series.
PS3557.R226Q4 1982   811'.54   82-17115
ISBN 0-89594-095-7
ISBN 0-89594-094-9 (pbk.)

To Marilyn Monroe
who tried, I believe
to help us see
that beauty has a mind
of its own

Acknowledgements

All my thanks to my research assistant and good friend Karen Sjöholm, who always seems to know what I am doing; for ideas, information and support thanks to Paula Gunn Allen; for her encouragement and research help for the foundation and beginning poems thanks to Wendy Cadden; thanks for encouragement from "The Girls" of Los Angeles and especially Eloise Klein Healy; for their encouragement I am grateful to Kate Winter, Michelle Cliff, Adrienne Rich, Audre Lorde, Deena Metzger and Luisah Teish.

Most especially I want to thank Bella Zweig Debrida for her six-week course on the subject of Helen as a Goddess; and for her help with Greek etymology, and for giving me the word and the concept of El-Ana.

Thanks to Bill Vartnaw for letting me hear his "Angel Poems"; to Marian Roth for last minute feedback, and to Olga Broumas for the use of her typewriter.

"The Inheritance" is dedicated to the memory of Joseph Cadden.

"Paris and Helen" is for Carolee Sanchez and Paul Vane.

"A dream of Helen" is for Clare Coss and Blanche Wiesen Cook, and of course for the quail eggs.

Some of these poems first appeared in magazines or anthologies including *Sinister Wisdom, Bread and Roses, Contact II, The Greenfield Review,* and *Spiders and Spinsters,* edited by Marta Weigle.

"The most blonde woman" is originally from *She Who* by Judy Grahn (1972) and collected in *The Work of A Common*

Woman (St. Martin's, 1980) originally published by Diana Press in 1978.
The poem is part of a short film on the subject of Mt. St. Helens by Fran Tonelli, *Silent No More,* 1982.

"The Inheritance" was hand-printed as a broadside by Toothpaste Press, West Branch, Iowa in concert with a reading given at the Walker Art Center, 1980.

"The land that I grew up on is a rock" is a chapbook published by Gorilla Extract, San Diego (Steve Kowit).

"The good weef" is a broadside produced by Stanford University in conjunction with the Women Writing in America Conference, April 1982. It was designed and printed by Cheryl Miller with a hand-colored woodcut.

"Spider Webster's declaration" is a broadside from Interval Press, San Francisco (Cheryl Miller).

The Triangle Fire story is from a book of the same title; also from *Labor Heroines: Ten Women Who Led the Struggle* by Joyce Maupin. Rose Schneiderman was the organizer who made a speech in a whisper; one hundred forty-three young women died in the 1911 fire, trapped because the doors were locked to keep out organizers. Hannah, Angelina and Ellie are names of my conjecture; one of the women did throw out her hat and the contents of her purse in a grand gesture before leaping eight stories.

Table of Contents

A Chronicle of Queens

I said in *The Work of a Common Woman* that I had written
the series "Confrontations With the Devil in the Form of
Love" after seeing the original stage production of Ntozake
Shange's *For Colored Girls Who Have Considered Suicide
When the Rainbow Is Enuf*... and that I didn't know where,
exactly, I was leading myself; just that I was going some-
where with the idea of using lyric poetry to express herstoric
narration: women's stories.

Now, six years later, I know where the new place is. It's
called *A Chronicle of Queens,* and *The Queen of Wands* is the
first of the set of books.

Wands will be followed by her sister, *The Queen of Swords.*
One poem from that series—"Queen Boudica"—has been writ-
ten and published in the *Iowa Review* special issue on women.
Swords will be followed by the passionate *The Queen of Cups*
(or Hearts) and then *The Queen of Diamonds.* Suits of the
Tarot are Wands, Swords, Cups and Pentacles. In the card
playing deck, they are called Clubs, Spades, Hearts and Dia-
monds.

Judith Rae Grahn
July 16, 1982

I first met the Queen of Wands

I first met the Queen of Wands in a 1913 translation of a
clay tablet of ancient Babylonian writing, that wedge-shaped
cuneiform record from the ancient Middle East that is like
the footprints of birds.

The text of the tablet, called "A Tablet of Lamentation,"
begins chillingly: "the cow wailed, and in her place she lay
down." The story is of a queen who has been stolen from
her temple and carried away by ship. "My temple thou art
not," she wails in grief. She has been stolen from her city,
her people and her land, by an unknown and unnamed enemy
called by her, "The Foe." Coming by ship, he strips off her
clothing and jewelry, and carries her away into slavery on his
vessel. This theme of a queen who has been stolen, of cities
and temples ravaged by soldiers, of people cudgeled in their
streets, of lamentation for a female power gone, is a repeated
one, especially among mid-Eastern cuneiform tablets of the
period around 2500 B.C.

Moved by the tale told in the Tablet of Lamentation, I
searched for other stories of stolen queens, wanting to iden-
tify this one with a name, occupation, some motive for the
theft. The most persistently retold story of a queen stolen
in Western tradition is that recounted in *The Iliad*. In this
story the queen is Helen, Queen of Sparta and known as
Helen of Troy, where a furious war was fought over her per-
son. Her face was later described as so beautiful as to be,
"The face that launched a thousand ships." She was hated
and blamed for the most famous war of western history and
literature, the model war of Troy.

In investigating Helen's story I found an astonishingly
worldwide myth of a female god of beauty, fire, love, light,
thought and weaving. She is a figure of many forms and
names and countries, and she is the Queen of Wands.

After identifying her as a weaver I was carried back, so far
back in time that an ancient spirit presented itself to me for

the purposes of my story. This spirit is a weaving spider, a fate spinner from whose very body comes the cloth of life and time and understanding. I named this spirit *webster,* or Spider Webster. Webster is a word that formerly meant "female weaver," the "ster" ending indicating a female ancestor, or female possession of the word.

The word-weavers of recent centuries who have given us the oration of Daniel Webster and the dictionary listings of Merriam-Webster stem from English family names that once descended through the female line. Some great-great grandmother gave them her last name, *Webster,* she-who-weaves. In this story of the Queen of Wands, webster is a spider/spirit, often quite immense (in the woods, the moonlight; peering over the horizon with a sun-like eye) albeit she is also often tiny, lurking in the corners and shadows of our all-glistening, aluminum world. If the webster of dictionary fame comes first to your mind when you see Spider Webster's name, remember that she gave the surname to him, as well as giving the words. For language is a form of weaving too, a clothing our ideas wear, a glowing flesh they are made of, a heart that beats in them.

I.

Gods and Heroes

All Greece hates
the still eyes in the white face,
the lustre as of olives
where she stands,
and the white hands.

from "Helen," by H. D.

Here in the sunrise

Here in the sunrise,
oh webster, is where,
intense,
I hear the singing
in, and of, the loom.
The web of light
like fingers, the
fingers like a shuttle
and the shuttle like a
bird, dancing.
It has all the meaning
we can make of it.

The land that I grew up on is a rock

I.

From my mother, a rock,
I have learned that rocks give
most of all.
What do rocks do? They hold the
forces of the earth together and
give direction. They interrupt
the mindless sky in its total
free fall.
Rocks turn the monotonous winds
from their courses and bring down rain
before the all-collecting sea
reclaims it—so you and your friends
can have some, too.
A rock is a slow, slow
cooled-off flame, and a cradle, both.

They are like bone, the rocks. They frame.
They remain. They hold you.
They grind together to make digestible dirt.
Because of their slow lasting
nature, they are said
not to feel tangible hurt.
We were star-struck, my father and I.
We ate fast intellectual pie.
And we made fun of her, my mother;
she made material, actual pie.

But once, in a flash of insight,
he said of my mother: "Without her,
people like you and I would fly
right off the earth."

He made a gesture of his hand helplessly
sucked into the sky (like a navigationless bird).
He knew she was a rock
and so did I. He knew the worth
of gravity and certain repetition,
the safety of enclosure.
I knew the mute, the flame-charred
female wall, the dam
of granite rock between one's child self
and the molten family core,
the hell of terror, the inner and the outer
fire: my father's ire.

II.

"You never listened to me."
Unexpectedly my mother weeps, recalling
how we never took her on our flights of thought
or left her, her own falling-out time.
How we locked her from our patch of
significant sky (that she was holding still for us)
my father and I,
as though she were a sheer wall of will
to be mined
to mill
and to grind and to be there
with or without our care.
It is so shocking for us
to see her now, a rock
weeping.

She is rocking
in her rocking chair
a little madly, deliberately deaf
to our star-struck talk.
She is chalk.

III.

This lasts only a moment, a few years,
for my mother's tears
quickly evaporate and
return to their own mother, the sky
who weeps intermittently over everything,
renewing
without care,
and with the greatest care,
especially over the rocks,
bathing and cooling them
who by their basalt nature
cradle their feelings for the
longest time and most profoundly,
taking continuous
though sometimes secret, pride
in what they give
and giving the most of all.

Whether we (sky divers) care to learn
how to share this treasure,
my mother's spirit will return and return
teaching us. Whether my father and I
will learn, or not.

"Your mother is a saint," he says.
He means,
the center of a rock, particularly
the one we live on,
is molten like a star, the core
is light,
enlightening, giving of
intelligence.
Stretched far into the cold unwieldy sky
my father and I
in reaching for a star,

we nearly overlooked the one
that pulsed, all that time,
there (beneath us)
under our floating feet, and *in* us,
in the person of my mother,
rocking sometimes somewhat madly
in her brilliance-giving vision,
as the earth,
a rock, a star.

History if I could put you

History if only I could put you
in my little bowl,
cherish for your real self
you, source of what follows
and goes before.

Flama. Name. Story.

History if I could smoke you,
suck you up into my brain's blood
like a memory
of what really happened,
all the sides of it
the middle, top and bottom
including the beautiful
the boredom
including the painful burning parts,
my own part,
wrong, right and indifferent;
wisdom and war, love and foolery.

History, little golden glow
of understanding
let me blow and blow
on your heart.
Tell me something.
Tell me truly.

The Tablet of Lamentation

The following is a tablet of lamentation from Babylonia, written down perhaps about 2500 B.C. in cuneiform writing, done with a wedge-shaped stylus pressed into damp clay sheets (*cune*, triangle-shaped). The narrative is addressed to a queen who is also a god with a number of descriptions and names. The name of a spirit who inspired the teller was evidently scratched out by a later censor and is represented in the text by three dots. The translation was by Stephen Langdon, in 1913, from *Babylonian Liturgies*.

The cow wailed and in her place lay down.
She wailed, the cow wailed and in her place she lay down.
Like a woman in childbirth wailing in her place she lay down.
Virgin of heaven (queen of) . . .
She that smites the mountains queen of Eanna.
The heavens she shakes queen of *giparu*.
The earth she causes to quake, queen of Eanki.
Lilanna   queen of sheep-folds.
Mother of Temples   Dada the holy woman child bearing
Nana . . .
The spirit the word of . . . was brought to me,
The spirit the word of . . . was brought to me,
The spirit the word of . . . was brought to me.

He came to my temple.
By the mountain road he entered.
In ships he came to me.
In ships he embarked.
The . . . entered . . . .
His unwashed hands upon me he put.
He with sandals entered.
The swift horsemen . . . came.

The possessions upon the prow of the ship he put.
I the queen upon the ship's stern rode.
The foe, he with sandals, entered my court.
The foe put his unwashed hands upon me.
He put his hands upon me, he filled me with fear.
The foe put his hands upon me, with fear he oppressed me.
I with fear was filled, but he did not dread.
My garments he tore away, and clothed his wife therein.
The foe stripped off my jewels of lazuli and put them on
    his son.
I tread now his courts.
So for me myself he sought in the shrines.
Then I was filled with fear. "Cause her to go forth."
Not should I go forth.
In my temple he pursued me, in my halls he terrified me.
Like a frightened dove upon a beam I passed the night.
Like a sudin-bird that flees from a cranny I hastened by night.
From my temple like a bird he caused me to fly.
From my city like a bird he caused me to fly.

"My temple is behind me," I cry.
"A queen am I, and my city is behind me," I cry.
To my temple, "My temple thou art not," thus I cry.
To my city, "My city thou art not," thus I cry.
To my habitation, "My habitation thou art not," thus I cry.
If I say I will not enter into it, its beauty consumes me.
If I say I will not come into it, longing for it causes me to
    tremble.

Even as he destroyed it, destroy thou him likewise.
Do thou thyself even so, make him ashamed.
Oh woman as in thy chamber thou didst perish,
Do thou even so make him ashamed.
Thou thyself the foe even so wilt requite.
Oh queen the foe even so thou wilt requite.
"I myself did not cause the shame; my father caused the
    shame.

The lord of the lands caused the shame; my father caused
the shame.
Where once I hastened not, I sorrowed not, now I shall be
glad . . . ?"

How long before her, how long before her shall my heart
be cast in gloom?
Oh virgin of heaven   queen of heaven.
Thou who shatterest the mountains, queen of Eanna.
Who makest the heavens to tremble, queen of the dark
chamber.
Who makest the earth to quake, queen of Eanki.
Lilanna   queen of Eturdagga.
Who lovest the temple, O Dada sacred woman child
begetting . . . .

from *Babylonian Liturgies*
translated by Stephen Langdon (1913)

The meanings in the pattern

The interior of the Arizona Indian museum
is cool. A woman stands at the counter,
selling her family wares. "I am a Pima,"
she says. "We have always been here.
People say, where did the Anasazi go?
But we are right here, we never left.
We were farmers, always.
We were promised water for our gardens,
now they are taking it. My daughter
made the baskets; only girls are taught
to do it. My son made this pouch."
She pats the small soft leather purse,
thick with close beading, red and white,
yellow and blue. The design: clouds,
a bird, a man, the earth.
"This picture tells a story," she says.
Her black eyes looking inward and outward.
"No one who buys this could ever understand—
the meanings in the pattern. What it is
really worth." Clouds. A
bird. A man. The earth. Her fingers
feel the beads. "There is a story here.
It takes three days and nights to tell it."

They say she is veiled

They say she is veiled
and a mystery. That is
one way of looking.
Another
is that she is where
she always has been,
exactly in place,
and it is we,
we who are mystified,
we who are veiled
and without faces.

A dream of Helen

1. The Tree speaks:

The sun is a wild pumpkin this Fall.
The still lake surface is a mirror,
and I can see myself reflected:
I am the fairest of them all,
elderly, tall, bedecked with leaves,
my round brown branches are
flung wide as arms
and I am waiting.
My roots are woven to the bank
whereby I stand
to watch the Swans come down
like gods
to light upon the crystal lake,
to land like beams of light
upon the surface of an eye.

I wait. The air grows crisp.
My leaves curl and dry.
I watch the sky.
Everything is perfect and perfectly
connected, from the humming
of the insects to the footprints
of the bears, at the base
of my spine.
I am certainly perfect, in my
prime.
The air, everything is so still,
it is so clear that I will hold him
in my lake-reflected arms, the one who is
the first one down.

The great Swan. I will hold him
while he dances out his message
on my wide-flung limbs
in that split second
just before the image breaks,
just before the gossamer, the
netlike water, tears
to let him in.

What symmetry of quality
that memory has
of what a lovely world
that was.

    2. The Egg of Being speaks:

My mother plucked me
from the great dance
of great birds
flying like stars, points
of light on maps
moving in the velvet wall
of night sky.
And I was called
the Daughter of Memory
and the Grandchild of Time.

My mother pushed me, wailing
from her yoni basket.
I lay in the wet green grass,
the perfect oval with a golden heart,
a world inside, a cluster
of amber possibilities, a
shell-cased spinner of flesh
and bone just waiting to be found,
to open, to be taken home.

14

My mother tied me
in her apron string, then
cut me from her cord
and let me go,
a perfectly knitted knot,
a wick.

My mother lit me
on her lap, an altar
and I was called the Flame
of Life, El-Ana,
gathering of forces
Beauty. Motion. Harmony.
Attraction.

My mother thought me
in one golden flash.
She had that kind of mind.
But I set out to do more
than think, to do the next
task, to break, to ask,
to find, be found, to ken,
and to do more than stand.
to understand.

Helen's names

Helen has such a lengthy history
as a god and as a queen
that her name, El-Ana, has derivations
and echoes that are widespread over
continents. The Muhammedan Venus is called
Anael, which has the syllables of
El-Ana reversed. From El comes Bella
meaning "beauty."
Beulah Ann is one variation,
as are Helena, Helga, Holga, Helda,
Hilda, Holde, Hillary, Helna, Hildegard,
Helle. Hlin. Hlinda, Linda. Honnele.
 Heleme.
Yelana, El-Inna, Lil-Ana, Lilly Anne,
Lou Anne, Lillian. Angelina.
 El-Luna, Elna, Elanya
Elana. Hannah Belle
Annabel, Belle Anna, Belana,
Helana, Elaina, Elaine
Eleanor, Eileen, Alienor
Hela, Nina, Lenora, Lee Anna, Leona
Nona, Ilona, Lena
Ellen, Ella, Ellie
Nellie, Nell. Hel-Aine,
 Helaine.
 Lena, Lana, Lanya
 Helanya.
 Hello, Helanya.

Paris and Helen

He called her: golden dawn
She called him: the wind whistles

He called her: heart of the sky
She called him: message bringer

He called her: mother of pearl,
        barley woman, rice provider,
        millet basket, corn maid,
        flax princess, all-maker, weef

She called him: fawn, roebuck,
        stag, courage, thunderman,
        all-in-green, mountain strider,
        keeper of forests, my-love-rides

He called her: the tree is
She called him: bird dancing

He called her: who stands,
        has stood, will always stand
She called him: arriver

He called her: the heart and the womb
        are similar
She called him: arrow in my heart.

One for Helen

What did the Greeks steal
when they stole Helen of Troy—
what was the loot, the beauty?
Was it only a face, some graces—
a sex toy?

Doesn't even she remember how she spun
twine from her woolly distaff, and strung
cords in a line with even spaces
on a wooden frame? And as she wove
the songs she sung were played upon
another kind of loom which has become
the fundamental harp. The music staff
unravelled from the weaver's staff,
the notes taken from the knots,
the shuttle reshaped into a bow,
the resinated strings—
all these were her things.

This was viola
da gamba, violin, cello,
the chamber with strings, the singing in
and of, the loom. From her room,
the wooden belly of her
chamber, came the sitar, twelve string
guitar, piano, banjo, kyoto,
clavichord and zither. The electric bass.
This (and not her face)
was the original, the real lute. The instruments
of Helen, when she was a poet,
a singer and a weaver.
She emitted so much music! in her work.
They heard. They pried open the door.
And these are only some of the things
they took her for.

Helen's lover

When he was a young man he had skin
that glowed like pollen, and
with his swollen blossom lips,
his afternoons of energy, his hips,
his dense leaf smell—
with such a spell around him of vitality
and certainty, how could I ever
say I'd never love him, who was like
Paris, in the springtime,
ship in my harbor, sun in my windowsill.
When first he arrived, the swell
of birdwings beating all around him,
there was a flutesong in his eyes;
'forever,' he whispered but even as
he spoke the pollen blew
forever off his lips, the ship grew
cannon, and then conquerous. Now the grown
man lunges up my steps, so armed, so
dangerous, drunk with a different
determination. Did he kill
the young man, simply, his body
left for dead beside me in
my house of smells, my beaten
birdwing feelings, my own body
beginning to weigh me down,
and for a mate, the heavy
hated one, the one who's treated me
a captive, the one I've treated
like a foe?

Queen Helen

A queen am I
Queen Helen is my title.
As the sun shines so shines Helen
most beautiful.
I am what ever is
the weaving tree
and Mother of my people

I was Sovereign of my homespun folk
with their sheepshorn woolly garments.
We were considered most ascetic,
most athletic and democratic,
and I was entirely settled in my queendom
with my husband and my child,
when one day a young man came by
and I was undone.
He had won a contest
with the gods. I was the prize.
I was the golden apple
he had won. He, Paris, took me home
to his own land.

"Husband I am leaving,"
was my song.

> Husband I am leaving you,
> have left. And my homeland,
> child, and precious people;
> all the wild, wild island
> of my queendom.

I believe it was a matter of the
time, of Fate, a cosmic binding
and unbinding.
Ties I felt to go
pulled harder than the ties
I felt to stay.
Had my power been slipping?

Did you get the message I had
pinned for you to see:
"I want my full measure of reality,
I don't want the numb illusion.
Only sightfulness can make us see.
Only freedom makes us free."

Foolish words probably,
of a queen wrenched from her earth,
a queen taking to the air,
a queen flying.
Yet I feel a new fertility . . .

I moved my queendom and my court,
my ladies and my special looms I brought
with me as well as the hearthfire
that was my totem,
"Heart of the sky,"
and heart of the house
of Helena at Sparta.

"Lilanna," Queen of sheep-folds
they called me,
who causes the earth to quake.
Mother of the temple
and of the people,
Nana.
A Queen am I
Queen Helen and a Sovereign,
Flama. Shaker
alike of earth and of the heavens.

Without his heart he ranted
thinking it was me he wanted,
thinking that he could not live
or rule without me.

And the women I left knitting
at his palace
needled and poked incessantly,
until his pride bled
and his whole brain broke.
Who does Helen think she is, they said,
to go among strangers,
and to let herself be prized
so highly, to be called "the fairest."
Haughtiest of dames and proudest,
has she never heard of "modest"?
Sitting in the Trojan tower,
does she think she has such power,
does she think she is a goddess?

> Here is what I know:
> Even the most golden
> golden apple sometimes
> rolls down the long wand limb
> and lands in the lap of fire.

In ships he came to me,
in ships surrounded.
I was dumbfounded.
A thousand ships, so many!
where had he gotten them?
They filled the harbor
like a bobbing forest.
I was almost proud;
I stood on the ramparts of the city
and exclaimed out loud.

None of us knew the war would
last so long
and be so boring.
None of us knew we women were already
in prison. We sat in the weaving room
month on month, winding the distaff,
working the shuttle,
with only our own housebound prattle,
with never anything fresh, not air
or news or love or food.

We entertained each other
with bawdy jokes and stories
and a tapestry that told the progress
of the war. We comforted the new
widows. The bone-torn mothers.
Subject we were to every nervous stew of
scary rumors. No one danced.
Almost, we lost our glow. Ten
years passed. At least the men
had action—however many bodies paid for it.
And we all held fast, somehow.

In the tenth year it was clear
that those from the ships
had lost. They quarrelled
and skulked and bled.
Stench of the burning dead
came to our noses even in
the weaving room.
And they had stopped singing at night
or calling out my name
in derision or admiration
or lust.

They had lost, their shoulders sagged.
They won battle after battle without
taking the city or getting near me.
We no longer lived in so much dread.
We waited for surrender to be said.
But they were unjust.

And they won it finally with a lie,
hypocrisy,
the offer of friendship
with soldiers in its belly.
They won it with
the lie, hidden under honey
like a razor in the bread.

I too fell for the lovely painted horse,
with his wide nose flaring.
I too wished to have a party and be daring.
Queen of morbid siege was I,
Queen only by my title,
and I too grabbed for the sudden win,
the grinning, golden bridle.
Forgotten were the lessons
of want and pain,
the bodies dragged round
the walls of our emotion.

He was glinting like the sun
or like an apple. He was
neither; he was a bomb exploding
in the last battle.
Years of boredom
and regret blanked out as
I reached to embrace, to bind,
to pull him nearer with his
sparkling, blinding cargo.

We cheered when we had got him
all the way in. And then he flamed
into a torch and tortured;
seared the city down to ash and
rubble twenty centuries could
not even find.
And I began to live the recent
history of my kind.

All that night
we clung in tiny groups together
watching Paris and every
other Trojan man
die, too shocked to cry.
Thousands of corpses, so many!
such a limp crowd. I stood on
the ramparts of the tower and
exclaimed out loud.

So Helen fell like a pretty city
into the lap of war, a husband's war
against her.

A queen am I, Queen Helen
is my title.
Queen at the heart of the greatest
Western battle—
they have said was all on my account.

They have said the war was on my account,
my "beauty," they said, as though beauty
is something someone else can capture.
As though the Flame transfers.

I went out a Queen
a Sovereign, Mother of my people
and a lover—

I came back a captive.
My husband had gone out
a King, a Sovereign
and a soldier.
He came back a tyrant,
a master of slaves—
and I came back a slave.

> For the first time
> when he put his hands
> upon me, I was afraid.
> I was positively filled
> with fear. He chased me
> through my own halls,
> even into my temple. I
> crouched like a frightened
> dove, passing my nights
> on the edge of my bed.

> Never had anyone felt so ugly.

I hardly recall the remainder
of the story; it dragged
past like a sluggish drug.
No one in the country used the
word "civil" anymore.
In the aftermath of theft and war
came more war, more blood
and sudden changes.

My sister had murdered her
child-killing husband on his return.
No woman blamed her, none
except her daughter Elektra.
And that was the one who mattered.
Elektra goaded her brother
'til he broke with rage and slaughtered
his own mother.

And me. I was not only a slave,
I was a murdered slave, by my own
sister's children. The old maternal
order flooded in blood the day
the two conspirators climbed
the steps to my jail tower.
It was my worst hour, and I hardly
remember it. They have said that
I did not die normally, but flew
into the heavens and became a star.
Venus? was it? Beauty.

      I have been trying for centuries
      to recall exactly why
      I left my original queendom,
      was it on such shaky ground?
      Downward bound?
      Why was I dragged back
      into such a state—
      Do I lie sleeping?
      Will I wake?

A Queen am I. Queen Helen
and a Sovereign.
Flama. Shaker alike of earth
and of the heavens.
a queen am I
Queen Helen is my title.
As the sun shines so shines Helen
most beautiful, most blamed.
I am what ever is,
the weaving tree
and Mother of my people.
and I shall be
the Mother of my people.

II.

Magicians

In the groin of the natural doorway I crouched like a tailor
Sewing a shroud for a journey
By the light of the meat-eating sun.

from "Twenty-Four Years," Dylan Thomas

The Inheritance

How we have each labored
to create this civilization,
most of us against our will,
without our knowledge, thrilled,
enthralled, appalled or stalled
in this industrial serfdom
known as 'modern man';
this card game with its temporary flush,
founded on the village skills of
ancient women and their men, distilled
drop by drop from all the liquors
of our many lives, that electrifying
amber glow, that aura of what
our bodies do and know,
that history we can tell and show,
so trivially classified as 'work'
and 'workers.'

Trivially classified, enlisted,
tagged—
brought from an old
Old Country
in small sacks,
the scientific-magic of our
former ages,
bagged like the wind
and sold, breath by breath,
solo by solo, riff by riff
and measure after measure, as if
it were all free, and not
accumulated treasures
of complex creatures
such as you, me. The wind.
A tree.

The grandfather wind, the
mother tree, the message
delivered like genes, like
green beans, or
language given to a child,
accumulated patterns to be
used or listened to, as recipes
or tools or principles,
the message
passed along a long wind, the
whistling of a dancing bird
upon a dancing tree: Nothing is free,
everything belongs to one another,
nothing begins new, everything has
a mother, a father and a story.

The good weef is both

The good weef is both
weaver and wife, those old
words meant the woman-as-a-maker,
not especially bonded
to one husband,
but to the Spider Woman of life,
the one with ties that bind,
knitter of the sacred, magic knots,
who with her scissors or her knife,
is tie-breaking life-taker,
queen of what-is-not.

Wife and weef and weaver,
she was the market-woman
of Europe. Ale-wife, she sold
the ale she brewed; oysterwife bawled
what from the mothersea she drew,
strawberrywife what she grew.

The fishwife brought her stinking
reputation with her to the modern ear,
reference, they say, to a certain smell,
said with a certain sneer. The smell is
of queens.

The midwife stands midway
between the laboring weaver and her weaving
and the world, easing the way to life.
I am pleased to call myself a wife too,
a word-wyfe.

Frigga with Wuotan

The physical principle
of energy is this: the flame
lives inside the wood
as the erotic charge
lives in my belly. He
comes in to get it
with his beautiful
magician's stick—the one
that is his own. He
says that I enflame him.
I say that we enflame
ourselves.
Rubbing the sky's electric wand
like this, in the groove
of the earth's soft woody substance,
to conjure some creative fire
is an old human trick;
tribe upon tribe
has arisen from it.

Frigga with Hela

Her fingers
within me
   a spindle
my feelings
   woolly
her dear hand
   axis
on which my internal world
   whirls.

"She is making me"
on the whorl of her love
turning me out and in
transforming patterns.

So I say of her,
"she is making me,"
and I mean she is
making me over,
again.

Knit the knot: a riddle

The directions said:
to knit the knot known and
not to knit the not known,
knit the knot known
to the unknown knot
and not the knot known to
unknot the unknown
and knot the knit;
to unknot the known and knit
the unknown, unknit the
knot known and know the knit;
to know how to not know
the unknown, knit the knot.
Gnaw your fingers to the bone
until you understand the plot.

Hela (Death)

In the South and in the West
the sun is a monster
eating your water, eating
the juice right out of your bones,
and blinding your eyes,
your brain.
The sun takes photographs
they say, burning a record
of the day's events
into the filmy leaves of trees—
those wise old women-sticks.
The middle of the sun is dark, an eye.
At Hiroshima, they say
the radiation was a white
storm, the center of a flash.
Some people who vanished
in it left their shadows
on the wall, a still life
photograph.
I am Hela. I am used for all
purposes. I do not care.
I clean down to the bone earth.
I sear. I flare.
I take photographs
of what is no longer there.

The Queen of Wands

And I am the Queen of Wands.
Okay.
Here is how the world works:

It is all like nets.
ever golden, evergreen
the fruits fall
into   hands-like-nets
the fish are hauled
into   jaws-like-nets
the insects crawl
into   claws-like-nets

and the thoughts fall
into   minds-like-nets
it is all like nets.

On the other hand
a spider lives in the topmost branches of a pine,
her house a god's eye gleaming among the needles.
On hot days
she pays out her line and
twirls on down
to the surface of the lake or pond
to get a little drink of water
and to wash her face. She's such an
ordinary person.

The trees line the earth, great and small,
dogwood, plane, maple, rubber,
the elegant palm. The scrubby oak. The elm.
We're ordinary persons, too. We have our
long time friends across the distances,
our urgent messages and our differences.

And we have our parties.
We sugar up our petals just to get the probes of bees in us.
Most green ladies love everything the whipping wind can
    give them.
The avocado tree hung with her long green breasts,
she aches for fingers pulling at her;
the cherry, peach and nut trees bent with swollen balls
long for hands and mouths and claws;
the fig tree with her black jewels tucked between her
hand-shaped emerald leaves, is happily
fondled by the dancing birds, wild and raucous and drunk on
natural fig wine.

almost any summer morning
sun beams fall into my arms like lovers
giving me everything they've got
and they're so hot   oh honey
I take it all

give it to me, baby
is my song

And I am the Queen of Wands.
The people honor me.
I am the torch they hold over their own heads
as they march march like insects
by the billions
into the bloody modern world,
over discarded corpses of their ages past,
always holding me, aloft or in their arms,
a flame in the hand of the statue,
a bundle of coals
in their inflammatory doctrines, calling me
a chalice of fire,
essential light,
the Flama
and the stuff of which their new world will be made.

Sophia (Helen) they call me, enlightenment,
"God's light," wisdom, romance, beauty, being saved,
"Freedom" and the age of reason.
Progress, they call me, industrial revolution,
"People's rule," the future, the age of
electronics, of Aquarius, of the common man and woman,
evolution
solar energy and self-reliance. Sexual self-expression.
Atomic fission, they call me, physics, relativity,
the laser computations in an endless sky of mind,
"science," they call me and also emotion, the aura of
telepathy and social responsibility, they call me
consciousness, "health," and love
they call me, bloom of Helen.
Blush upon her face, and grace.

And here I am a simple golden shower.
and here I am only a spider
webbing their minds
with pictures, words, impulses
feelings translated into moral imperatives
and rules for living, like leaves
upon a tree, spread to catch the sun's attention.

They (the billions of people)
dance like Fairies on my smallest
twiggiest branches
whistling in each other's ears,
collecting and dispersing
seeds, wearing gold and
pretty clothing, worrying and not
really noticing all the other worlds
around them
how the sun center of my eye sews them
how the silver dream filaments direct them,

how their own thoughts connect them, how
the baton smacks their knees to make them
move their feet, that baton
at the end of the claw
of the Queen of Wands

And I am the tree
with candles
in its fingers
the tree with lights
Menorah
Yule-flame
tree of life

the tree-shaped
candle-holder
on the mantle
on the altar
on the flag of being.

And I am the Queen of Wands
who never went away
where would I go?

the flame is central
to any civilization
any household

any bag of bones. Any motley mote
you've got, of
little mustard seed can grow
into a yellow spicy flame
as you must know.

The sun is a weaver
and the rock earth her instrument.
Slender-fingered threads of light
and heat, dance like birds
shuttling.
Winds and the rain,
seeds and feet and feathers
knit the knot
making the great coat,
the coat of all colors.

The coat of all colors;
over the whole earth, a caught fire
of living logs, brown and red,
tan and white, black and yellow
bobbing like a forest;
each a magic stick with
green flame at its tip

a green web
my leaves, my green filaments
like fingers spread
to catch the sun's attention, spread
to catch the sun like thread,
like sexual feelings, like
the gleam from an eye, or an idea.

and I am the Queen of Wands
I am who stands
who always will
and I am who remembers
the connections woven, little eggs
along the message line.

I remember giving dinosaurs
to the tall unfolded ferns to entertain them.
and immortality to the cockroach.

I remember the birthday of the first
flower, and the death of so many furry
animals and kinds of people, and a star
that fell. I remember a continent
of green
green wands of grass
burning into the knees of
buffalo queens, a landlocked
ocean of fire. Replaced by the
picket fence. Almost equally complex.
Sky scrapers like spikes.
But that's another song.
And I am the Queen of Wands
who burns, who glows, who webs
the message strands,
who stands, who always will.

Helen your beauty: a chorus

Helen your beauty—
is it a meteorite? or
is it as cold, and
is it as tight, and
is it as gold
    as gold?

Some things are dry goods
some are wet
some are to covet
some to get.

Helen your beauty—
is it your blush,
is it innocence?
what is untouched—
or is it what touches?

Helen your beauty—
is it what gives, or
what is blamed,
is it what lives, or
what is enflamed—
or what flames?

Helen your beauty—
is it emotional?
a hot-flush
or a rush?
Is it a halo or a psychic glow,
Helen your beauty—
is it your soul?

Helen your beauty—
is it as light, and
is it as bold, and
is it as bright, and
is it as old
     as gold?

The most blonde woman in the world

The most blonde woman in the world
one day threw off her skin
her hair, threw off her hair, declaring
"Whosoever chooses to love me
chooses to love a bald woman
with bleeding pores."
Those who came then as her lovers
were small hard-bodied spiders
with dark eyes and an excellent
knowledge of weaving.
They spun her blood into long strands,
and altogether wove millions of red
webs, webs red in the afternoon sun.
"Now," she said, "Now I am expertly loved,
and now I am beautiful."

Helen in Hollywood

When she goes to Hollywood
she is an angel.

She writes in red red lipstick
on the window of her body,
long for me, oh need me!
Parts her lips like a lotus.

Opening night she stands, poised
on her carpet, luminescent,
young men humming
all around her. She is flying.
Her high heels are wands, her
furs electric. Her bracelets
flashing. How completely
dazzling her complexion,
how vibrant her hair and eyes,
how brilliant the glow that spreads
four full feet around her.

She is totally self conscious
self contained
self centered,
caught in the blazing central eye
of our attention.

We infuse her.
Fans, we wave at her
like handmaids, unabashedly,
we crowd on tiptoe pressed together
just to feel the fission of the star
that lives on earth,

the bright, the angel sun
the luminescent glow of someone
other than we.
Look! Look! She is different.
Medium for all our energy
as we pour it through her.
Vessel of light.
Her flesh is like flax,
a living fiber.
She is the symbol of our dreams and fears
and bloody visions, all
our metaphors for living in America.

Harlowe, Holiday, Monroe

Helen
when she goes to Hollywood
she is the fire for all purposes.

Her flesh is like dark wax, a candle.
She is from any place or class.
"That's the one," we say in instant recognition,
because our breath is taken by her beauty,
or what we call her beauty.

She is glowing from every pore.
we adore her. we imitate and rob her
adulate   envy
admire   neglect
scorn. leave alone
invade, fill
ourselves with her.
we love her, we say
and if she isn't careful
we may even kill her.

Opening night
she lands on her carpet,
long fingered hands
like divining rods
bobbing and drawing the strands
of our attention,
as limousine drivers in blue jackets
stand on the hoods of their cars
to see the angel, talking

Davis, Dietrich, Wood
Tyson, Taylor, Gabor
Helen, when she goes to Hollywood
to be a walking star,
to be an actor

She is far more than a product
of Max Factor,
Max Factor didn't make her
though the make-up helps us
see what we would like
to take her for

her flesh is like glass,
a chandelier
a mirror

Harlowe, Holiday, Monroe
Helen
when she went to Hollywood
to be an angel

And it is she and not we
who is different

She who marries the crown prince
who leads the processional dance,
she who sweeps eternally
down the steps
in her long round gown.
A leaping, laughing leading lady,
she is our flower.
It is she who lies strangled
in the bell tower;
she who is monumentally drunk and suicidal
or locked waiting in the hightower,
she who lies sweating with the vicious jungle fever,
who leaps from her blue window
when he will, if he will, leave her

it is she and not we
who is the lotus

It is she with the lilies in her hair
and a keyboard beside her,
the dark flesh glowing

She whose wet lips nearly swallow
the microphone, whose whiskey voice
is precise and sultry and overwhelming,
she who is princess and harlequin,
athlete and moll and whore and lady,
goddess of the silver screen
the only original American queen

and Helen
when she was an angel
when she went to Hollywood

Calumet (The Pipe)

The long cool stone pipe is her body,
its bowl is her vulva. Man-spirits flutter
in the tied and dancing feathers.
The mound of glowing tobacco
is old Grandmother Kundalini
who burns at the base of our spines.

The people pass the pipe each to the other
in communion, sucking the sacred breath
of smoke through the long tube
as a god spirit might suck a breath of
energy up our backbones. It is a
beautiful event, a breathing.

And it is a message nearly lost,
a cost in blood to thousands
of tribal peoples.
We may believe
"tobacco" is the reason
for colonial actions;
the real fight is for the pipe,
the flama.

When some modern Indian men
misused the fire of Calumet
for their own advancement
recently, the keepers of the pipe,
the clan elders,
took the power of the pipe
back into themselves.
For three years she will not be used.

As the jewel of life rests
in the purse of safekeeping
so their brown hands
shield her sacred substance
from all sight.
They will not contribute
to her abuse.
They prefer her sleeping. Or.

They prefer her sleeping.

In the tower of the crone

The small town streets were neat
and orderly the day I met the hag.
She was trying to catch a cab
to the downtown drugstore, illicitly
to fill her morphine habit when
she spotted me.

The hag smiled, blue eyes bleary.
What a disheveled, needled thing
she was, coat worn
over a pink slip, hair rank,
a nest of unremembered chores.
I pitied her, stared at her gold teeth.
I was sixteen
and avid for adventure.

She held my unassuming face.
"What beautiful expressive eyes
you have," she said. "You ought
to be a star, an actress."
I was bedazzled. "I was an
actress once," she said. She laid
her hand upon my arm.

And I became apprenticed, following
her home. Not to a tower, exactly,
though a jail: a square hole
with unmade bed, crawling with cats
and flies and maggots, open cans of
catfood stinking everywhere.

My whole heart bled.
Still, I stayed. I put her to bed.
"I played with Ethel Barrymore,"
she said, "and dear John, on the stage
and in the movies."

My mother punished me when I got home.
Forbade me to return to the old crone.
But I was in a trance, nevertheless,
a success-trance. I too would tell
tales on the American loom.

A month later I read of the once-known
actress found dead, after three days,
in her room. And I learned:
  the price of first is last
  the price of fire is ash,
and don't go into the weaving room
alone, alone
don't go into the weaving room
alone.

Spider Webster's declaration:
He is singing the end of the world again

He is singing the end
of the world again,
he has sung it before.

When he flattened Troy to the ground, seven times,
left Carthage salted like a fat old hog,
Africa, "conquered," he said, he announces,
he is singing the end of the world again,
millions burned in Europe, butchered in
Africa, millions blown to bits in China,
Russia and now in Central and South America,
thousands of tribes
and villages destroyed, the matrix
of whole peoples, cultures, languages, genetic
pools, ways of describing, gone, gone,
apparently, according to his song, whirled up into
his description of the past.

He is singing the end of the world again,
he has sung it before.
Americans fly over their world and its ghosts,
Americans stare at their own ghosts without
recognition. Invisible the Indian ancestors,
invisible the Mayan-centered
feather industries, invisible the
great buffalo and the buffalo queens,
old ladies of the hip high buffalo grass,
invisible the engineering systems, amphitheaters,
philosophical wholeness in the old
civilizations of the mind.
Occasional sulky sacred bears
stare from the cages of zoos
refusing to acknowledge men as their children.

He dwells in threats of fire, Armageddon, Hiroshima, Saigon,
and Tyre, Berlin, Gomorrah, Hell itself,
the story of fire, his theft of it. "Put
a large wad of flame on
the wand's tip. Wave it,
shouting: Fire, Fire."

The whites of their eyes stare
back at him.
There was a city *here* once, once
there was a city (and now there
is another)

There was a tribe
and now there is another,
there was a nation here once
and now there is another.

He is singing the end of the world again.
He has his song
and I have a long, long
wand like memory.
I remember five worlds
and four have ended.

I see (I can't help it)
buffalo faces in the gloomy white
people of Iowa, waiting slump shouldered
for the light to change,
chanting, "We used to rumble the earth here,
once, with the charge of our electrifying
hooves. Now in the midst of the stolen
golden corn
standing in their fields like sacred groves
surrounded by plenty we are oddly depressed."

He is singing the end of the world, again.
Reincarnated bears
prance and sway in the lowlife bars of
this place calling itself a nation; they
lean, pissing, on the wall in Dallas,
Detroit, Charleston, Denver, hold intellectual
discussings in great roars,
knife each other, make predictions.
They await the Bear god, the Bear Maiden. They
are not concerned with the form this will take,
it is their form, they will take it.

Dancing birds leap out of the young faces
kissing on the streets of San Francisco, Salt
Lake City, Memphis, leaping with an urgent
sky-message; and the lovers call what they
are feeling, "love," "desire," "relationship."
They do not know to call it,
"Birds dancing."
Birds *do* dance, and so do
ghosts, and buffalo.
Spirits line shoulder to
shoulder on the highways shouting
Maya   Azteca   Aztlan   Olympus
Mississippi Valley   Seneca Falls   Cibola
Shangri-La,   The River Niger,   Hollywood,
Tibet. Atlantis. Eden.

There was a nation here, once
and now there is another.
Business people pat each other's pinstripes,
putting their own names on the ancient remedies and
products, systems and understandings. "Let's
design a rocket out of here. Don't forget to
bring the queen of buffaloes. It gives me such
satisfaction knowing she is mine. Let's pretend
that we are doing this for sex,
for money."

He is singing the end of the world again
he has done it before.
He has his firebrand
and his song.
I have a long, long
wand like memory.
I remember five full worlds
and four of them have ended.

III.

Soldiers, Workers and Gods

Sun
make me whole again
to love
the shattered truths of me
spilling out like dragon's teeth
through the hot lies
of those who say they love
me

from "Chorus," Audre Lorde

Lamentations from other Babylonian tablets

"For Ur destroyed I weep with many tears"
"For the temple I weep, even I weep"
"Like a sheep-fold harrassed, her heart laments."
"The plain with lament she fills
    with lament, yea the plain with lament she fills."
"Now as in the days of old where shall I go?"

For the city, alas, the treasures, my soul doth sigh
For the city Lagash, alas, the treasures, my soul doth sigh
In holy Girsu the children are in distress
Into the interior of the splendid shrine he pressed
The August queen from her temple he brought forth
O Lady of my city, desolated, when wilt thou return?

Then the fair wind forsook the city, the city lies in ruins.
(O father Nanarra) the city has been turned to ruins;
the people are lamenting.
Under the tall gate where once they walked, dead bodies lie
On the broad streets where they rejoiced in festivals, they were
overrun by the wicked
On all the streets where once they walked, dead bodies lie.
On all the places where they rejoiced in the festivals of the
    land,
people lie in heaps;
The blood of the country has been spilled like molten bronze
    or
lead from the pot,
Dead bodies have melted like the fat of lambs put out in the
    sun.
They bite the dust like a gazelle smitten by the spear.
Woe! Women wallow in their own blood at the place where
    they gave birth.

The cudgel has killed many, they lie, their heads unbandaged.
The lance has killed many, there they lie unbandaged.
People are reeling though they partook of no heady drink.
Whoever dared resist, arms have cast down; the people are
    lamenting.
Whoever fled, the storm has swept away; the people are
    lamenting.
In Uru the strong and the weak have perished of hunger.
Old men and women who stayed in their houses were
    destroyed by fire.

from the Sixth song of the Sumerian poem,
"Lament on the ruin of the city of Ur"
(2000-1000 B.C.)

61

But I mean any kind of thief

When I went
looking for the Foe
I called him "he"
the one in the fast
car and the outside lane,
the getaway man
who came and took
and went, a stranger

but I mean any kind of thief—
of souls, pride, the heart,
of land, space, air and work.
I mean the thief of truth
of meaning

the one who goes
by what is said
and not by what is done
that one
that kind of liar
the fantasizer

smoker of bad wishes;
the cold one who, shivering
steals your thunder and your fire
then calls you poor,
calls you "Queen of Wants"

and wants.

When I went looking
for the Foe I thought of

boots and leather, barbed
wire fences, aggressive
legal stances and the
colonizer
who takes the heart
out of your sky, diverts
the light from your eye
into his own

but I mean any
kind of Foe, her, the
sap-sucking cannibalizer,
idea-eater, and the one,
the ones who make war
with rents and wages

the masked mate,
who makes war with love
and personal rages
the raper who takes
your sense of self
and wholeness,
flame of trust
and leaves you trembling,
crusted with his fear.

the daisy bringer
who calls you Queen for a Day
and takes your year

the friend who cries on your shoulder
and never sees your grief
who looks in your mirror
and calls you low
and calls you less
than who you are
I mean the Foe
that one
I mean any kind of thief.

Webster, I've seen you spread your sturdy web

Webster, I've seen you spread your sturdy web
of derelicts and winos disguised in
doorways of the downtown business districts of
the cities where in the midst of all
the flashing traffic, your dark eyes
stare and stare
searching the faces of the secretaries
for a trace
of her face, her flare, her
particular godlike confidence
and grace.

Old Helen

Discarded in old town, bunched,
wearing indigo-blue
worsted leg veins,
you were a beauty once,
Helen, weren't you—
before the ships came.

You were a beauty once
before the ships came
to your (oh oh) rescue,
bearing gifts or promises or chains,
field labor or the mills,
warping you with pain,
debts or deadly chemicals,
spinning your beauty down
to an empty spool in old town.

You were a beauty once
Helen, a singer and a weaver,
spinner and a storyteller too,
of greatest fame,
before the ships came.

Now your face shows
what you have had to know
about the use of beauty,
youth, flying fingers too
(where they fly to).
You know the first name of the booty
they got, and as you lug
your burdens down the street
with no one to help you,
you remember what they mean by "rescue."

You were a beauty once
Helen and you will be.
Your expressions prophesize.
The anger migrates through your veins
like great flocks of flesh-devouring
birds, wheeling and diving, gathering the drives
to unknit the terrible pattern of our lives.

When I went looking for the Foe

When I went looking for the Foe
I could not find him.

I mean,
when I went looking for the Foe
I found him trying so hard
to be the Queen,
the mother, source.

I don't mean impersonating,
that's another kind of Queen,
a flaming queen.
I mean replacing.

I hated, and I understood.
Women know their wombs are mysteries
who operate on dreams,
a loom or flax seed
given to an unknown weaver
from an unknown mind.
Spider Webster's, no doubt.

What's a poor Foe to do?
When the *queen* is equal to the power.
Stealing's the prerogative
of those who have not got
and have no other way to get.

Now we know the meaning of
he wants.
He wants me, and of me, and
he steals to get it,
what he has not, himself,
got. Then he can be "who gets,"
a god—
and I can be gottess.

Like a woman in childbirth wailing

A queen am I
my city is within me

ever and ever did I swell
with its messages
delivering all it ever needed
to know of itself
cell by fleshy cell
and spark by spark
and all entirely in the dark.

I plied on the smallest, starkest loom
inside the smallest, darkest room
knitting fingernail to finger
iris to eyeball to socket
I rarely missed a stitch.
Almost the hardest thing I had to know
was when to call the baby done
and let it go

nor did I have to lug the burden
by myself

     I, when the wind spirit
     swole me up
     sisters surrounded
     to hold me up.
     Ours was the whole birth,
     and the power of blood
     and the bread and roses.

     Ours the riddle of the ring
     releasing even as it encloses.

Ours the molecules of flesh
on the helix spindle
ours the spinning of the whole earth
with its knots and bundles.

Ours the word
when the word was spoken,
ours the zodiacal belt,
the axis moon, the time of month,
the herb tea taken.

Ours the babe
when the womb was open,
ours the singing, the chants,
the counting string,
the new fate woven;
ours the circle that remained
unbroken.

And then one day the Foe came.
He with his forceps.

he with his forceps
to replace my muscles, his
pincers, metal instruments
instead of grandmother's long fingers
and my midwife, whom he killed.
Who he destroyed in such tremendous
numbers. Tied and tried. Condemned.
She stood high in the flames
like the Queen of Wands
her faggots blazing all around her.
How we wailed when she was burning,
hiding, running, our child's eyes
from the fleshfire turning.
He called her a witch,
he with his mask and swords.
But I did not stop him

He was so clumsy then
He tied me up and
turned me upside down
to birth against the force of gravity,
sewing me back together like a doll
because I ripped, I tore, my organs
dripped down my legs in my old age.
And if they spoke of this at all,
the mothers to the daughters
spoke with rolling eyes, in horror;
and when I complained
he drugged me for the pain
so then my babies choked at birth
of overdosed brains,

> Oh how long, how long before you
> must our hearts be cast in pain,
> o queen of heaven, queen of the dark chamber,
> Lilana, queen of sheep-folds, Nana queen of childbirth
> holy woman, child begetting . . . .

a queen am I
my city is within me

ever and ever did I swell
with its messages. And now
he is passing me by.
like a man
in a myth
I now give birth
through my side, my belly,
gut sliced open to accommodate
his glove—while I lie passed
by, unconscious, thieved
of all my beauty—my volition.

No wonder they call it
Caesar's operation.
Still, it saves lives.
That is the hook
he has me on.

This industrialization
of love, of birth,

this is the last besieged castle
the last tower
and of this particular war
this is the last hour.

the great, pink walls
of this genetic treasure cave
are being shaken
and this will be the final city
ever taken.

Blow, whistling wind, blow
the filament of
breath that stirs the feather
from within the egg, the cave,
the place of birth, the city

built of flesh, the muscular
enclosure, bag of skin
that holds us in and gives us rest
and motion, meaning and sweet
method. Oh womb, cell spinster,

as you know
the only real production *is* love.
I mean the ties between all unlike beings,
minute connections on
the message line, the one continuous knotty cord

(oh spider webster) wrapping us together.
I mean that esthetic, feeling-chested
glow, electric field of quickening,
the envelope of thought
and feeling dropped
over the still flesh
like a golden, animating net.

a queen am I
my city is within me

it seems that
he and I are joined
to make another
kind of being

and what I call "make"
he calls genetic engineering.

He reproduces flesh, metallic
organs, miles of pumping blood
in plastic veins, hormones in
powder form; he transposes parts,
his a factory womb, producing
factory beings, healed and cut
with laser beams; someday
I will have removable
dayglow-colored viscera
in soft purselike plastic.
I can give my heart away
quite literally.

    The cow wailed
    and in her place lay down.
    Like a woman in childbirth wailing,
    she wailed, the cow wailed
    and in her place she lay down.

72

May there be a breast
to nurse my child
and may there be
a chest to hold my heart
and ears to cup my words,
and may there be a bird
to dance my story.

Chains

After he took
my fire to be his own

He turned the thread of life
connecting us
into a complicated chain.
He thought to bind me
for his purposes.

I wanted to tell him,
to say this can't go on,
This isn't really him,
this isn't me.
Nobody listened.
I changed, then

I, who had been a tree
with stunning branches
spreading like a love god
for all life to live itself in
went stunted, standing in a line,
millions of times, producing
in a limited way, burning up and
burning out and
on my way to ash.

He changed also.
He became concrete and leaden,
his mind making only heavy metal
linkages
as he ringed himself around
to hold me fast
and fastened.

(He who had been a bird, eons ago,
a bird, dancing)

It has been many centuries.
I called him the other day.
"This arrangement can never last,"
I said.
And it hasn't.

Beauty, sleeping (Who shall wake us)

Who shall wake us
if we don't ourselves
shake loose the sleep
of ages, animate the doll
at last and bid her
rise, and move and rule.

Who will wake us from our
dream of capture
if we don't ourselves
shake loose the long spell,
the illusion of being small
and silenced, sourceless
and unheated.

Who will be all knowing
and the prince if *we* don't
make him happen, somehow
groom him for his task
to rouse us from the suicidal
slumber.

(And the Foe if no one else
knows how to shine his boots
knows how to stride
to the tower steps
and rocket up to shake us
from our sleepy lives
with fear. But I don't mean
the Foe, I mean another
and ourselves)

Let the prince come
integrated and sure
let it be time
for a man strong in his
insides
without boots or
a broken brain, let him
have a golden net
around him

Let him arrive now
in any form, as a Bear God
or computer programmer
or even a dyke in a man's costume
let his step resonate the steps
of the hightower

Mothers mothers raise him
tell him, make him
who will wake us
who will wake us
who will wake us from our
trance of ages
if we don't

Ourselves prepare
for that reception;
animate the doll's flesh
for the kiss of life
of recognition,
animate the doll's will at last
and bid her rise
and move, and rule

Grand Grand Mother is returning

The egg is always being made
and making,
always getting laid
and laying;
thread is being spun
and spinning,
truth is being found
and finding,
getting all unwound
and winding,
being all unsnarled
and snarling,
and the Grand Grand
Mother is returning

that's all I know

Don't suppose it will be
as it is remembered
in time past

time present is a different
unpredicted
picture

time future happens
only in the mind

Worlds are always ending
and beginning,
tales are getting learned
and learning,

birds are always taking off
and landing;
the sky is ever being turned
around, and turning;
the tree is ever being stood upon
and standing;
and the flame is getting burned
and burning

Grand Mother is returning
don't expect
the past, expect
whatever happens,
men are moving, more
than ever women are
just wakening;
Grand Grand Mother
is returning

that's all I know

Helen you always were / the factory

1.

Spider:

Helen you always were
the factory

Though almost wherever you sat placid,
bent at your creative toil,
someone has built a shed around you
with some wheels to oil, some owner
has put you in the shade to weave
or in a great brick box, twelve stories,
twenty, glassed, neonic and with cards
to time your time.
Though he has removed you from your homey
cottage industry, and made you
stranger to your own
productions, though he titles you his worker,
and himself your boss, himself "producer"

Helen you always were
the factory
Helen you always were producer

Though the loom today be made mechanic,
room-sized, vast, metallic, thundering;
though it be electric, electronic,
called a mill—a plant—a complex—
city of industry—

still it is a loom, simply, still just a frame,
a spindle (your great wand) pistons and rods,

heddle bars lifting
so a shuttle can be thrown across the space created
and the new line tapped down into place;
still there is a hot and womblike bucket
somewhere boiling up the stuff of thread
in cauldrons, and some expert fingers dancing
whether of aluminum or flesh; still there is
a pattern
actualized, a spirit caught
in some kind of web
whether it's called a system
or a network or a double breasted
cordless automatic nylon parachute
still it is a web and
still it comes from you
your standing and your wandish
fingers, source, your flash of inspiration,
your support, your faith in it
is still the fateful thread, however it is spun,
of whatever matter made.

And still it is the one true cord,
the umbilical line
unwinding into meaning, transformation,
web of thought and caring and connection.

Just as, Helen you dreamed and weaved it
eons past, just as your seamy fingers
manufactured so much human culture,
all that encloses, sparks
and clothes the nakedness of flesh and
mind and spirit,
Helen, you always were the factory.

2.

Hannah:

Flames were already eating
at my skirts,
and I heard one of the girls
behind me screaming just how much
burning hurts. I could see the
people gathered on the sidewalk.
Eight stories high
I stood on the ledge
of the Triangle building
and exclaimed out loud.
Then I took my hat
with its white and yellow flowers
and flung it out, and opening
my purse, I scattered the coins
I had earned
to the shocked crowd.
Then, I took Angelina's hand in mine.
I thought we should go down
in style, heads high
as we had been during the strike
to end this kind of fire.
I grabbed Ellie's fingers to my right;
her clothes were smoking
like a cigarette, my little sister,
so serious, seventeen,
actually gave me a clenched smile
just as we leaped, all three
into the concrete sea.
We fell so far.
We're probably falling still.

They say a hundred twenty
thousand workers
marched on our behalf;

they say our eulogy
was delivered in a whisper;
they say our bodies
landed under the earth,
so heavy we became,
so weighted as we spun down;
they say safety conditions changed
after we were killed.
Because we fell so hard
and caused such pain.
Because we fell so far.
We're falling still.

3.

    Spider:

Helen you always were
the one enticed

The one consigned
to leave your pile of clothing
by the river while you
bathed your beauty
and were stolen. Always
you are the one thrown over
the shoulder, carried off,
forced to enter the car, the plane,
the bed, at swordpoint; lined up,
loaded onto the ships and
shanghaied, tricked
out of your being, shafted,
lifted and held hostage,
taken for a ride.
Always you are the one
coerced to sign the bad
contract; ordered to work past sundown;

the queen riding the stern
of her once proud ships,
serving two or ten or twenty years
before the mast,
cheated of all pay at last,
and thrashed by the birch rod,
the cat-o'-nine tail wand.

Helen you always are
the coals stoked
and taken from the hearth,
the precious flama
spilled upon the floor
and blamed and blamed
for the uproar
when the whole house
goes up in smoke . . .

4.
    Nelda:

We were marched to the coast
where the ships waited.
I remember their masts, tossing,
—the pain of loss,
of being lost—
like spikes, through our hearts.
On the passage over
we were stacked like logs
below the deck, our fragile
and our sick
thrown to the fiery sea.

My whole family died.
My husband, my beloved child;
my village, my past life
became a dream.

I barely existed
when I arrived.
For who was "I" to be alive?
Like a lone star
through the blue sky
falling netless
to a new world. What
was new about it was our terror.

But we kept our memories.
We kept our peoplehood, our past.
And oh good god
we stood. We stood in
water to our knees, to plant the
seeds, we stood in ashy fields
and picked the ill-gotten
tobacco and the cotton and
the sugar beets and all the sweet
sweet meats we could never eat.
The sun a dragon.

We spread out
a network to Detroit, Chicago,
Newark and LA, all over the land
for the assemblyline work,
getting blistered in the oil-slick
city streets, scalded in the kitchens
and the laundries, fired in the
fires of hard times. But we did
much more than just survive; we scarred
and healed and sealed and shared and spieled
and blared and smoldered,
joining—however knotty it may be—
our memories
our dreaming and our wand-like hands,
to burn together like a great black
brand. A dance of fire.

"Remember dreams, remember Africa,"
we sing, and what we mean
is freedom, wholeness,
that integrity of being
that chooses its own time, its
own kings and queens.

5.

    Spider:

Helen you always were
the bag of life

You with your carriage,
the yoni-weaving basket
with the belly-drag,
the well-used pouch,
the cookie jar indefinitely
filled and emptied.

Helen you always were
Santa's fat sack,
full of little worlds
to hang on the great
green tree, so prettily.

Helen you always were the belle
of the ball and the ball
of the bell
with the golden heart,
the egg yolk
of we human folk.

The singing music box
composing magic children
with their sticky
democratic fingers
in your eyes like wands
in water.
The ship's hold stuffed with cargo,
a carving of your image on the bow;
the white sails strung along your arms
like everyday laundry.

Helen you always were
the honeycomb
the honey and the honey jar
kept open by the bear's claw
and the words, "we need her,"
and sometimes even, in your nightmare,
the harried wasp who hurries
to lay her hungry eggs
before they hatch inside
and eat her

Helen you always were
the factory
Helen you always were producer

6.

    Nancy:

Do you see the boys lined up
to board the ships
to ride the tanks
around the walls?

The flint-faced fathers
with their scanners
and their maps,
the saplings on the firing
line, woven in the mat
of war, to be rolled out
on any shore
to batter after
every door,
to lie in lifeless lines
across the warehouse floor—
is this the pattern
that I labored and I bore,
the blood for blood, the arms
for arms, the heart
torn out
to hurt some more

And who am I

if it is me
they say
they do it

for?

7.

    Spider:

Helen
you always were
the egg laid
by the golden goose,
the full pot, the fat purse,
the best bet, the sure horse
the Christmas rush
the bundle he's about to make;

the gold mine, a house of our own
the ship come in, the next stake,
the nest egg, the big deal, the steal—
the land of opportunity
the lovely lady being
luck and love and lust
and the last chance
for any of us,
the reason that he's living
for, Helen you're always
high card, ace in the hole and
more, the most, the first and best,
the sun
burst
goodness   quenching every thirst
the girl of the golden golden golden
West,
desire that beats
in every chest

heart of the sky

and some bizarre
dream substance
we pave streets with
here in America

8.

    Annie Lee:

Oh hell yes! I stand,
have stood, will stand;
my feet are killing me!

This tube of lipstick
is *my* wand,
this pencil and this emery board,

this mascara applicator
brushing black sex magic
from a bottle
these long fingernails aflame
with hot red polish, and
these pins, these sharp
spike heels, these chopsticks,
this letter opener
this long handled spoon,
this broom, this vacuum
cleaner tube, this spray can
and this mop,
all these cleaning tools
for sweeping, for undoing knots,
these spools and needles, all
these plugs and slugs and soldering
irons, these switchboards and
earphones and computer boards,
these knitting tools for
putting things together,
these are my wands.

In the parade I'm the one
in bangles and short skirt
twirling the rubber-tipped
baton; this is my umbrella,
and my parasol, my fan,
these are my wands
and oh hell yes I stand

I am who stands
I am also who sits
who greets   who wipes
who notices, who serves,
who takes note
and I am who stoops
who picks and sorts

who cuts and fits
who files and stores
who seals and bonds

and I need my wands
and oh hell yes I stand,
have stood, will stand,
in lines, in queues, in rows,
in blocks, in crowds, in basic
traffic pattern flows.
I have my wands, my hands,
my ways of understanding
and my family strands.

And here in the sunset
is where I like to hear
the singing
of the loom.
The strings of light
like fingers and
the fingers like a
web, dancing. It has
all the meaning
we have made of it.

9.

    Spider:

And still it is a loom, simply,
still just a frame, a spindle,
heddle bars lifting
so a shuttle can be thrown across
the space created
and the new line
tapped down into place;

still there is a hot and womblike bucket
somewhere boiling up the stuff of thread
in cauldrons, and some expert fingers
dancing . . .

Still it is the one true cord,
the umbilical line
unwinding into meaning,
transformation,
web of thought and caring and connection.

Just as, Helen you dreamed and weaved it
eons past, just as your seamy fingers
manufactured so much human culture,
all that encloses, sparks
and clothes the nakedness of flesh and
mind and spirit,
Helen, you always were the factory.
Helen you always were the factory.
Helen you always were the factory.
Helen you always were producer.
Helen you always were
who ever is
the weaving tree
and Mother of the people.

IV.

Notes

I have noticed that as soon as you have soldiers the story is called history. Before their arrival it is called myth, folktale, legend, fairy tale, oral poetry, ethnography. After the soldiers arrive, it is called history.

—Paula Gunn Allen

Helen as a Goddess, El-Ana,
Keeper of the Flame, House of Fire

Until recent times, an annual festival honoring Helen as an ancient creation God was held on the Greek island of Rhodes. She was worshipped and represented in the form of a tree. In Hebrew tradition she was Ashera; for the Ainu people of Japan she is Ashketanne-mat; for Sumerians she was Anait.

The birthday of the sun is winter solstice, December 21. In northern climates she is celebrated as the tree with lights. The blessed Mary's mother was Anne or Anna, Grandmother of Christ on his mother's side, the distaff side of the family. Ana means life, source, womb. Sometimes the word is *ama* instead of ana. The Sun Goddess of Japan is Ama-terasu. Hannah-hannah means the Grandmother in Chaldean. Hame Haa is a Pueblo Indian word, "in the place of the Grandmother," meaning time eons past, "long ago so far."

In various languages ana means life, altar, sustenance, grace. Ana means womb, and most of the words applying to woman and to the female Gods mean womb. *Gyne,* the Greek for woman, is the base of the word queen. Venus, beauty, means vulva. Ana-Yana-Yoni-Ioni-Gyne-Cune-Cwen-Queen.

In Tuareg tribes of North Africa, still matrilineal in descent, the title for mother is Anna, and for daughter, Yell. Anna-yell, Ana-el, El-Ana, Helena, "beauty." The Sun Goddess underlying Greek culture was Helen or Helena and she was much much older than Greek civilization.

El-Ana, Flame-womb, House of Fire, Thought Woman. El, creative fire, is present in words such as electric and element, and also in Ilium (the city of Troy), city of the Sun, Ile. On this continent, the Lakota Indian word Ile (Elay) means Flame. The Biblical God was originally Elohim, a collection of mixed spirit forces, before becoming merged into a single masculine figure, Yahweh. El, and Baal, Ile, Helios, Allah, became the names of masculine Gods after the Sun Goddess fell from power—something She did only in some parts of the world. To other people she is still the supreme creatrix or medium for reaching the other spirit forces. The story of her descent—the Fall of the God of Light—her capture and her still-living presence is primary in Western tradition, from *The Iliad* to *Cinder Ella* to *Faust* to modern movies of tragic female stars who rise, fall, are murdered, rise again.

A few other names for the Goddess of weaving, loveliness and fire are Oshun (African-Brazilian), Chin-nu (Chinese), Kochinninako (American Indian), Arani, the fire-stick (India), Ashketanne-mat (Ainu-Japanese), Venus (Roman), Ninnlil, queen of childbirth and Lilanna, queen of sheep-folds (Babylonian).

Yellow Flowers for Oshun

Oshun is Goddess of love and beauty in West Africa and in the African-Brazilian Macumba religion. (North American Voodoo practice calls the Goddess of love *Erzulie*.)

The color sacred to Oshun is yellow and her metal is gold. The food special to her and which members of her priesthood, her "children," are forbidden to eat, is the pumpkin.

Her earthly domains are inland waters, rivers and streams, the gentle waters. Her star is Venus, star of beauty. Her physical property is the mirror, sparkling jewelry, the fan. Her internal domains are the heart, love, beauty, flirtation, fickleness. These qualities are mentioned in the Tarot for the Queen of Wands.

Oshun in Africa is Goddess of the Niger River region, where she is held responsible for a devastating and important war that once took place there—provoked over her beauty. Her husband/consort/lover is Shango, God of thunder and lightning. She is fiercely jealous and protective of him.

Oshun is one of four major Macumba female Gods. The others are Obatallah (creation), Yemanja (the ocean), and Oyá (storm-fire warrior). It is said that when the crescent moon and the star Venus appear together in the sky, that is Oshun and Yemanja, talking.

Chin-nu, Heavenly Weaver-Woman

Chin-nu is the name of the Heavenly Spinster, or the Spinning Damsel of China. The traditional stories say that she was one of seven heavenly fairies, that is to say, stars, who customarily came to earth in order to bathe and play in a particular stream at the south end of a particular meadow. A cow and a herdsman lived near the meadow, and one time while the fairy weavers were bathing, the cow gave the herdsman a little underhanded advice.

"If you go and steal one of the fairy dresses," said the cow, "you can gain one of the fairies as a bride." The young man decided to do this, and proceeded to sneak up to the stream, hiding himself in the brush as he got closer to the piles of fairy clothing the maidens had left on the bank. Sensing his presence, the fairies rushed out of the water as he leaped from the brush to seize one of the dresses.

All except one of the fairies grabbed up her clothing and flew back to the heavens, where they live as stars in the constellation Lyra. The one left behind, Chin-nu, was known as the Weaver. Not having possession of her dress, she could not return home, and so had no choice but to follow the herdsman and become his wife. The Weaver-Girl and the Herdsman are said to have been twelve and fifteen years old when they married.

During the next few years Chin-nu bore a son and a daughter. She repeatedly asked her husband to reveal where he had hidden her fairy dress. He refused at first to tell her; then finally after she had asked and asked, he let her know his secret hiding place. She immediately got her garment, put it on, jumped into a cloud and returned to her place in the sky.

In the Korean version of the story the Herdsman is a prince, and his bride is called the Spinster. They both went into the heavens and were assigned apartments in constellations opposite each other in the sky by Yu-ti, husband of Chin-nu's mother. Chin-nu is constantly weaving garments for the family of the Heavenly Emperor while the Celestial Herdsman must stay on the other side of the Milky Way, far away from her in the constellation Aquila (Eagle).

The two lovers are allowed to meet only one day out of the year. This occurs on the seventh day of the seventh month, and then only if the pair can figure out how to cross the long, dangerous Milky Way. Chin-nu accomplishes this by making friends with magpies, who make a bridge of their wings for her to walk across the sky. And on this special day it is said that all the magpies on earth disappear for one day, and go to the sky to help Chin-nu and her lover, who meet on the east side of the Galaxy. The celebration of the festival of the seventh day of the seventh month is also held in Japan, where it is called Tanabata Festival, and where the Heavenly Weaving Princess is known by the name Orihime. On this feast night poems are displayed, written to her and to the Herdsman who captured her.

Chin-nu is also called the Stellar Goddess, the Spinning Damsel and the Star Vega, which is the brightest star in the constellation Lyra, the Lyre. Sometimes one of the stars is identified as her shuttle. She has also been identified with the constellation Cygnus, the Swan.

"My garments he seized," the Queen lamented in the Babylonian tablet telling how she was stolen from her land, and the Fairy Weaver of China, Korea and Japan must have used the same words; and so must many another woman, amazed when a young man takes her mound of clothing from a river bank, or from a drawer in her bedroom, or stages an elaborate pantyraid on her dormitory.

Ko-chin-ni-na-ko,
Yellow Woman and Whirlwind Man

For the Keres, an American Indian tribe, yellow is the color for women, and women wear it ceremonially. After a woman dies she is painted with yellow face paint so Grandmother Spider will be certain to recognize her as a woman in the other world.

For Pueblo people, Yellow Woman, Kochinninako, is a major figure, a representative of all womankind. One story they tell about her goes like this:

And Kochinninako was the most beautiful woman in her village. One morning she was grinding corn with her three sisters when they ran out of water, so she took the jars down to the river to fill them, after saying to them, "I'll get it." Bending over calf-deep in the cool water she had filled three jars when she heard a low voice behind her. Startled, she leaped around. There stood a large bear-sized stranger.

"Who are you?" she called sharply.

"I am Whirlwind Man," the fellow replied calmly, "and I have come to take you home with me, Yellow Woman."

"That's impossible," Kochinninako replied, setting her filled jar upright on the bank. "I have too much work to finish this morning and my sisters expect me back with this water." She gasped then, for the man had reached out and grasped one of her wrists.

"Get out of the water," he said, "because now you are coming with me."

"No!" she hissed into his face, yanking back with her hand. "My husband and my child expect me to make their dinner, and then my mother is coming over." Her voice stopped as she saw that Whirlwind Man had a long Bowie knife glinting in his other hand.

"How much more are you going to argue?" he asked.

"I believe I'm going with you," Yellow Woman said. "Just let me get my moccasins from the bank."

Whirlwind Man took Yellow Woman miles away from her own home village, to a house in the wilderness where he lived with his own mother, who greeted the beautiful young woman courteously, and gave her a warm supper.

For days Kochinninako stayed in that strange place, and every day she said to the mother, "Please, I must go home—won't you help me?" For Whirlwind Man had taken her clothing and hidden it so she could not escape.

One day the mother said, "Very well, I will help you. Wait just four more days and I will make dresses for you and for your three sisters. So saying, the old woman wove and stitched and knitted and embroidered until she had produced the four loveliest dresses Kochinninako had ever seen. And these she took back with her to her own village where they were very glad to see her again.

Now when a woman goes off for a while to be with a man, leaving husband and child and family to wonder and to worry for days and to have to go to other relatives for supper and a bath, when this woman comes home there will be trouble. There will be tears and gossip and censure underneath the joy of seeing her return safely. There will be a great deal of talking behind her back, and little discomforts. But after a while of the subterranean tension, someone will begin to set her story in place, to set it in time. The time of the Grandmother, mythic time. "She must have been Yellow Woman," they will say. "And she couldn't help herself. No matter what she wanted, Whirlwind Man took her." And then everyone will understand. And the gossip, the bad talking, will stop. And her life will go on.

Spider Grandmother: "Heart of the Sky"

In the north of Japan live a tribal, spirit-force worshipping people known as the Ainu. Particular elements of their religion and its related stories are similar both to Sun-worshipping Scandinavian tribal folk stories and also those of certain American Indian peoples.

The Ainu religion is based in spirit forces named *kamui*. (Pueblo Indian fairy-spirits are called *gamiosh*.) For the Ainu, as for the oldest European traditions, the bear is the most powerful and spiritually-charged land creature. But their most important kamui is the natural force of Fire, the Fire Goddess, Fire-Sparks-Rise-Woman. And like so many Indian tribes, the Ainu worship a kamui who is Spider Grandmother, the weaver who controls many other natural forces and has been of supreme importance to human beings.

According to *Songs of Gods, Songs of Humans*, a collection of Epic Ainu poems gathered together by Donald L. Phillips, Ainu women worship spider goddesses (*yaoshkep kamui*) and spiders are companion spirits for female shamans.

Ashketanne-mat, "Long-Fingered Woman," is the name of Spider Goddess. Her long fingers help her assist women in childbirth, which is one of her many functions.

In one Ainu story, Spider Goddess enacts magic to get rid of an unwanted male intruder. Knowing that the foe, Big Demon, is on his way to her house, she establishes her helpers around the room: Chestnut Boy, Needle Boy, Hornet Boy and so on are their names. Then having readied her apprentice fairies, she turns herself into a reed stalk and hides from sight, waiting.

When Big Demon arrives Spider Woman's magic helpers soon drive him away: Chestnut Boy explodes in his face when he pokes the fire, Needle Boy pricks his rump, Mortar Boy thumps him on the head and so on until he flees in total disruption. Spider Woman meanwhile has not had to raise a single long finger of her own.

On the American continent many Indian tribes consider Spider Grandmother their oldest and most venerated deity. Among Pueblo tribes She is Thought Woman, who sits thinking all the meanings and paths of Fate we human beings then proceed to act out. Because She thinks, we are. Her thoughts are like a psychic net dropped over the universe, as if a golden apple were spun into the tiniest possible molecules of light, electrons of inspiration and dropped over us as a universal mind, one we enter in psychic and dream states, and through which knowledge passes to us.

Spider Grandmother currently lives in an underworld place, Shipap, waiting to be called on again in this which is the fifth world of memory, as she was called upon ages and worlds ago before human beings decided to go their own way without her. Other worlds of human beings have come and gone, destroyed by tumult and flood, indifference, misuse of the god spirits, and greed or obsession with the solely physical and mechanical. But Grandmother Spider goes on and on with her long-fingered memory. She is Time itself, especially stellar time and the Milky Way.

Grandmother Spider brought the sun, spinning it out of her own substance and calling it her daughter, Golden Corn Woman, *I'yetico*. And Spider Grandmother brought fire for human use, being the only persona in the universe who was not afraid of it, according to a Cheyenne story. Poor Vulture tried to bring the fire back with him, and that is why he is singed bald to the neck and has scorched wingtips. And other creatures tried to bring the fire back but only Spider Woman, the fourth to try, succeeded with her tiny clay bowl for carrying the precious, glowing coals.

Traditions on both the American and Asian continents say that Spider Mother's grandson was given fire by her, or that he borrowed it or even stole it, and misused it, ending an entire world and driving the people to live underground, the earth being unfit for life. Hopi stories say the Spider Clan once ruled but that they misused fire by trying to melt the Arctic Circle and this caused vast upheaval and flooding.

Mayan tradition says Spider Grandmother is the Sun, and that her title is Heart of the Sky.

Magic and Sex and Weaving

"Spinning flax is my game, and Rumpelstiltskin is my name."
Magic and creativity and weaving, sex and weaving are connected in
the English language and traditions, in the songs and yarns. "When I
was a bachelor," the weaver sings, "I lived all alone, I worked at the
weaver's trade. And the only, only thing I ever did that was wrong,
was to woo a fair young maid."

"Tell her to knit me a cambric shirt," the singer asks in the song,
Scarborough Fair, "a shirt without seams; and then she'll be a true love
of mine." This has been interpreted to be a secret reference to the va-
gina—a cloth with no seams being a "perfect round," "the ring that spins
and has no end," being a riddle about a woman in the act of fucking.

"O t'was in the month of June when the flowers were in bloom,"
another song chortles. "I chanced to take a walk about the farm. There
I met a pretty miss and she promptly asked me this: 'Oh, won't you
spin my little ball of yarn? Ball of yarn, ball of yarn, Oh, won't you
spin my little ball of yarn?' "

The male weaver of legend is a sexual being, magical, likely to speak
of his semen as gold pieces spilled into a young maiden's "apron"; and
likely, like the Fairy people who were prodigous weavers, to take child-
ren with them when they went back to their homes in Elfland, or El-
phane.

Spinster is a word that has kept its history as a name for women who
do not marry, who are sexually self-determined and even lesbian. In
China women who work in the women-developed silk industry bribe
their way out of marriage, and are notorious as "bad girls," militant or-
ganizers and lesbians. They are true spinsters, defending the traditional
economic independence of ancient women.

The arts of weaving, including word/weaving, have become mechan-
ical and industrialized in factories. Yet these arts are still a primary
way for single women to earn money and be able to make a choice be-
tween marriage and spinsterhood—whether the factory is fruit-of-the-
loom, levi company, the garment districts, modelling, fashion, clothing
sales, working in the music business, the book industry, word proces-
sing in offices or "weaving" the tiny boards and chips in electronics as-
sembly plants. All these industries spin back in time to a group of
"heavenly" weaving sisters sitting at their looms—under the linden tree,
under the pine tree, under the chinaberry tree, under the piñon tree, un-
der the plum tree, under the palm tree, under the betel nut tree, under
the oak tree.

The Scandinavian and old North European Great Spinning Mother, Frigga, or Frigg as she is also called, had, as her name indicates, both male and female lovers spinning her ball of yarn. Her male consort was Wuotan (Odin), a thunder-god. She also consorted with a goddess, Hela, her converse and Mistress of the Nordic nine worlds of the dead. Hela rode in a chariot pulled by cats. The Tarot shows the Queen of Wands, in fact the entire Wand court, with cats.

Frigga's Ladies

Frigga, ancient Scandinavian Queen of Heaven, is Matron safekeeper of ships and navigation. A Fate-weaver, she spins on a dolgen distaff whose wheel is visible to us as the belt of the constellation Orion.

Friday is named for her, *Frigga's daeg,* the luckiest day of the week to her worshippers. Friday is the day dedicated by the Roman astrologers to Venus, Love-and-Beauty.

Frigga, or Frigg as she was called, is pictured as a whirling sun in conjunction with her mate, Thunder-god Odin (Wuotan). She has three Maids of honor, and all of their names are similar to that of El-Ana, the original Queen of Wands. But their functions are those of other Queens. Fulla has charge of Frigga's jewels. (She is a Queen of Diamonds.) Hlin cares for those in need. (She is a Queen of Hearts.) And Gna is Frigga's messenger, a horserider. (She is a Queen of Swords.) Swords.) The Mistress of the Norse Underworld is Hela (Death). Her domain is called Helheim, located under a magical tree of life and light, named Yggdrasil. Famine is Hela's table, Anguish her territory and her hall is called Elvidnir. She is the necessary obverse side of Frigga's life-inspiring character, for without death there can be no heat, no motion or renewal.

An Icelandic Tale

Once a man named Darad, a native of Cuithness, saw a number of wild looking horseback riders galloping furiously toward a large rock outcropping. They appeared to disappear into it, and Darad was driven by curiosity to follow. Coming close to the rock, he found an opening, and peering within he could see twelve gigantic, wild women who were all weaving at a loom. They sang as they wove. By squinting his eyes he could see that the weights of the warp strings in the loom were not stones but severed heads of heroes; the cross-string wefts were intestine strands and sinew; and the women were using arrows for shuttles and a sword for a heddle-bar. And as he listened to the lyrics of their song he began to understand that they were Valkyries, and the web they were weaving was the web of the life of himself, Darad. When their song was finished the women ripped apart the fabric they had made, mounted their horses and galloped away, some going north and some south.

Sleeping Beauty

Pueblo Indian Aunties of the Clan come to the naming ceremony when a baby is three weeks old. Clan Aunties of Medieval Europe who came to a baby's naming were Fairy Godmothers, or Grannies.

The Godmothers who came to Sleeping Beauty's naming ceremony did something peculiar. They "forgot" to invite one Granny. And this Godmother was utterly enraged to be excluded from the festivities and the all-important naming of the child, which helped determine its Fate and place in the village social order. Seething with jealousy, she swore an oath of vengeance to herself, that her own influence on the girl would come to be the most vital and important of anyone's. And so she stayed home in her tower and waited; and when the sixteen-year old came, she pricked her finger on a magic spinning wheel and fell into a trance.

A proverbial prince is usually credited with awakening her with a kiss. In earlier versions of the story, however, she was raped by a king as she lay sleeping, and gave birth to twins. One of them, searching for a nipple, sucked out the poisoned splinter. Helen's mother, Leda, bore twin boys and so, too, on the American continent, did the granddaughter of Sky Woman, first Creator of the Iroquois people.

Today, little girlfriends around the ages of eleven, twelve and thirteen play a very special social game. They get together in a group for a party or special occasion, whispering and eating and telling stories. And they very deliberately exclude from this gathering one girl they all know by not inviting her. And then they use her as a focus for gossip and judgment. They are certain to let her know that this is happening, so that it makes her extremely jealous and angry. Sooner or later she will pay them back.

Helen of Tyre and Simon Magus

Simon Magus was the greatest magician of the ancient world, performing such astounding feats that thousands of his followers considered him a god. The Emperor made up a plaque stating his sacred powers of divinity, Simon the God. He is said to have been the primary person responsible for preserving the Egyptian-based knowledge and understanding of occult astrological matters in the form of the Tarot deck, cards still used for divination by hundreds of millions of people.

Simon Magus was everywhere accompanied by a beautiful woman, a woman who was known as his Shakti, his source, and he said himself that all of his powers came from her, that without her he could do nothing. She was Helen of Tyre. Simon had bought her from a brothel where she worked as a prostitute in the cloth-and-dye making city of Tyre, renowned for its fine weavers.

Simon Magus and the beautiful card-playing Helen were worshipped as Gods in the area, sometimes being compared to Zeus and Athena or Hercules and Selene but mostly called themselves. Simon was called the Sun, and Helen was known as Helen with the lamp. Their worshippers were referred to as Simoniani and Heleniani.

Simon said that Helen of Tyre was the Word Incarnate, and that she had had a hundred reincarnations, in one of which she had been Helen of Troy. He called her, "She who stands, and will stand." He said her God name was Epinoia, "Thought," and that she was like Sophia, Goddess of Wisdom. Worshippers of Simon and Helen practiced free love, believed in sexual inspiration and licentious practices. They taught that Helen was "the lost sheep" who needed to be found; and that an individual was to be saved because of the grace that is within him and not by his works. Works are "just" only by social convention while grace is a timeless quality.

Simon and Helen taught that fire is the first principle, "power without end," and that it is an intelligent being (rather than the "devouring fire" God was for Moses). They said the Fire, Helen's Fire, the Flama, is that "which stands, which stood and yet shall stand." Every person has this fire inside, however tiny, and it can be developed in each person to its own immensity. This tiniest point of fire potential in each person is known only to the spiritual, is the kingdom of heaven which lives within us, and is the same as the seed of yellow mustard. But if the mustard seed, the image of the Standing One is not developed within the person in a lifetime, it will not survive the death of the body, which, like a tree that bears no fruit, will be cut down and cast into the fire.

The power that Helen confers, Simon said, is one power, divided into within and without, above and below; it is self-generating, self-increasing, self-seeking, self-finding, being its own mother, its own father, its own sister, its own son, being an abstract unity, being the root of all things.

Simon and Helen lived in the time of Jesus and many other prophets and magicians; and although in 220 AD their followers were still telling how they were able to raise the dead during the mystic services they held under the plane tree, many people ultimately rejected Simon Magus and Helen of Tyre as gods, instead turning to the powers and the image of the dying King who lives eternally.

The Conquest of Weaving

"Robe-trailing Trojan dames," Homer described the women who were carried away in ships to work as slaves. Descriptions of garments, dyes and cloth were high praise in that world much more than in this one. Sappho rarely exclaimed over another woman's beauty without including some comment about her manner of dress, that it was handmade from an island famous for its fine designs and craft, or that she was wearing especially handsome sandals, or that her mother understood the high fashion of wearing a purple ribbon in one's hair.

The clothmaking industry was primary. In brilliant, world-influencing Egypt, the rulership passed through the female line and the economy was solidly in women's hands—as it still is in many parts of village Africa, whose "market women" carry on a lively merchant trade. In ancient Egypt men did much of the labor and craftwork while women did much of the management, and the basis of the economy was the trade in clothing, cloth, and precious oils for perfume, body lotions and incense.

The Trojan War represented a shift in power: the Greek soldiers who won took skilled labor, especially the valuable weavers, back with them as slaves. And in a world without refrigerated trucks, airplanes or interchangeable mechanical parts, only a few kinds of goods were suitable for long distance trade. Bolts of cloth, rugs, "dry goods" were primary, the major means to the accumulation of wealth. So the capture of a handful of Trojan women tapestry-makers, "tapists," was the capture of an entire economic world.

And this is what the Greek men were doing, raiding weavers from their own islands and from the North of Africa. Ulysses could sell an ordinary worker for four oxen; a skilled weaver brought twenty oxen, five times as much. This is about the difference (on a modern wage scale) between a motel maid and a nuclear physicist.

The Romans continued the conquest of weavers from North Africa and Europe, building a vast military empire from the acquisition of goods produced by conquered tribal peoples. In Medieval times the tapestry and related arts passed into the monasteries and abbeys. Magic powers were still enough vested in the weaving craft, however, that the Inquisition went to great lengths to sever this connection by persecution.

Fear of spiders, spirits and Fairies was instilled, especially in the women of Europe, so that the magical connections that came from the earlier shamanic traditions were broken. This prepared villagers to eventually become workers in the mass production of garments and rugs that had lost all their storytelling, all their fateful meanings, all of Spider Webster's thinking, all the divinatory, astrological, tribal village patterns and symbols and meanings. No longer would the babe's swaddling blanket tell the story of its future life as predicted by a coven of thirteen Fairie godmother Aunties of the Clan. No more would the pattern of the wedding tablecloth or place-rug be cleverly designed to snatch a protective spirit from the air and hold it in geometric bondage for the safekeeping of the house.

In the future, garments would be mass-produced in an industrial world of short-term, disposable meanings. But to reach this stage, the old powers were first and very violently broken. Village wisewomen were accused of having "familiars" if spiders, mice, cats or owls were found anywhere near them, and the penalty was death. A house clean of all outside creatures meant a house safe from the flames of judgment and the Inquisition. Little European girls learned that when a spider sat down beside Miss Muffett she had better run away. Miss Muffetts who did not run grew up to be witches and were publicly burned.

Weavers were burned as witches as fervently as were midwives and healers—and thus the magical, tribal and essentially, historically female functions of those occupations were taken away from them. Barbers (surgeons) and owner-manufacturers replaced the power of covens, village guilds and abbeys. Although the actual closework continued to be done mostly by women, the control of the value, use and meaning of the weavings passed into the hands of men—a new kind of men—industrial men.

She Fell Like Lucifer from the Sky
(A Seneca Account)

European tradition says that the God of Light, the archangel Lucifer or Lugh or Loki, was cast down out of heaven, that he fell from power—and that, in dying, he became the star Venus. As a morning star Venus is called Lucifer. Lucifer means "light bringer." Related women's names are Lucell, Lucille, Luanne, Lucianne, Lucia, Lucinda and Lucy in the Sky with Diamonds. In ancient Rome, the Goddess of Childbirth was Lucina.

On the American continent, Iroquois tradition tells also of a God, Sky Woman, being cast from heaven. The creatrix of the Iroquois is Sky Woman, who fell, like Lucifer, from one world into another.

Sky Woman lived in a world far above this one, once, and she contracted a mysterious illness. No one could cure or help her, though many tried. Finally her father, a Chief of the people, said she could only be helped if a certain tree, the Tree of Life and Light, was dug up. So a large hole was dug under this precious tree which gave the people its fruit on which they lived, and which gave the people sunlight from its white flowers, enabling them to see.

They laid the sick woman beside the hole they had dug. But then a bad tempered young man came along. "Why should this wild cherry tree, so vital to us, this tree of our life, why should it be dug up on her account?" And so saying he kicked her and rolled her down the hole. The hole opened into the sky, and she fell into blue space.

Grabbing the tree with one hand as she fell, she plummeted through the sky with no place to land, until at last far below, some large water birds looked up. In some stories, these were swans. They were amazed to see a woman clutching the Tree of Life and falling through space.

"Let us receive her," they said, and so saying the water birds spread their wings under her and broke her great fall with their own feathery bodies. And to give her a place to be they dived and pulled mud from the bottom of the primeval sea, piling it high on Turtle's back to make the land. And so there was new land, in a new place.

After a while Sky Woman bore a daughter, who grew to womanhood strong and intelligent from eating the wild potatoes she and her mother dug. Then one day the West Wind got into her, and she became pregnant. She bore twin boys, but instead of acting as brothers ought toward each other, they quarreled. One of them, Sapling, was handsome and kind and brave. The other one, Flint, came out through his mother's armpit instead of the normal place, and she died as a result. Flint caused great destruction and trouble everywhere he went, and he was not loved by his grandmother, Sky Woman. She favored the wand-like Sapling; and after many conflicts the two brothers fought a terrible battle in which the ugly Flint was destroyed.

Straw into Gold

Spinning straw into gold involved colonizing the clothmaking industry, of changing it from a cottage, home-based trade into a centralized, highly specialized, mechanized enterprise.

The material resources were already there: tweed and serge from the Celtic tribal folk, felt from the Mongolian tribes, plaids from the Scots, fine linen and lace from Flanders and from the Irish, calico (Kali's cloth) from India, silk from China. Silk was expensive because of the arduous task of feeding tons of patiently picked mulberry leaves to the voracious silk worms, whose cocoons are boiled in vats to make a sticky mass that can be spun out into delicate spiderlike threads. So priceless was silk in China that the nature of its manufacture was kept a closely guarded secret for centuries. Japanese silk manufacturers acquired it in a traditional manner: they kidnapped four young girls, silk workers from China, and forced them to reveal the process.

Bolts of cloth have traveled everywhere, establishing a basis for trade and a reason for the colonization of territories. As the weaving trade became industrialized in Europe, coal mines were opened to feed the fires of the mills. Working conditions were extremely harsh, and living conditions for all the common people deteriorated in the crowded cities that grew up around the mills.

People in areas that had not industrialized were often coerced into raising sheep for wool for the mills, or food to be shipped in to the urban workers and their managers. The Irish potato famine was a consequence of this situation. The Irish raised plenty of fresh food but all of it was forcibly shipped to England's mill towns. The Irish people ate mainly potatoes, being too poor to afford the wealth of food they themselves raised, and when the potato crop failed, the people starved—one quarter of them. Bodies of the starved, it is said, simply fell along the roads. Another quarter of the people fled to America to look for jobs in American mills, to try to get American land.

American immigrants were to a great extent fleeing the drastic results of industrialization of manufacture in their original countries, the loss of their land, the harsh exploitation of their labor, the persecution of their minds and traditional village customs and values that had lasted through the period of their serfdom.

In America, the northern mills mechanized rapidly, competing with Europe, and demanded raw materials for the spools and vats and wheels of their production—especially cotton. Millions of African people were stolen from their villages in the fifteenth and sixteenth and seventeenth centuries, sold into slavery not for their fine weaving skills but for their bodies, to be field laborers in the raising of cotton, and also for the raising of other crops: the highly stimulating industrial foods—coca, chocolate, sugar, coffee, tobacco. The mill workers of every description would come to use them daily, even hourly, to artificially maintain high continual efficiency and alertness so they could keep up with the monotonous energy of the machines, the dangers to life and limb of the snarling metal, and so the production quotas could be speeded up until every drop of creative spark was taken from them. They left work utterly drained.

Workers fought in every way they could to wrest back a little something for their own lives. Germany was an early scene of weavers' strikes as people tried to get 18 and 16 hour work days down to 14 and then 12; and tried to get pay that would provide more than rude gruel, potatoes and unheated ragged quarters.

When the English colonized India the soldiers broke up the weaving guilds and forced the skilled weavers to work all day on their own land raising cotton for the voracious English mills.

The spillover from Europe's difficult and often slave-like conditions came to America. America became a golden dream, an idea of freedom and beauty and plenty for everyone. Immigrants from Dublin, Hamburg, Stockholm, Warsaw, Nepal, Shanghai, Corsica, Peking, Venice, the Philippine Islands, Korea, Madrid, all have believed the dream of "gold" in America. People saw gold in the Southwest pueblos on the Rio Grande, gold in the wheat and corn fields, gold in the California mountains, gold in the slave trade, gold in running rum and cocaine and laudanum, gold in the yankee mills and in Chicago, gold in the fur trade, the alcohol trade, the prostitution trade, the land trade, the railroads, gold in the Chinese labor camps, gold in mining, gold in Fort Knox, gold in gambling casinos, gold in the stock market, gold in Hollywood, gold in Florida oranges, gold in California sunshine, in the bright lights of the city, in blonde, blonde women. In America, gentlemen prefer gold.

Gossamer

In "The Tree speaks," "gossamer" is the exact word. There is a partic-
ular season of the year when baby spiders are born and "balloon," a
method of travelling in which they let out a long streamer of thread
that allows the wind to blow them high in the air and carry them miles,
even hundreds of miles, from their original mother's egg sac. This sea-
son is called "goose summer," in German, "gossamer," and hence the
"gossamer" which has come to mean the shimmer created by the light
reflecting from the spider streamers.

Credits and Bibliographic Notes

The Tablet of Lamentation is from *Babylonian Liturgies*, translated by Stephen Langdon. Special thanks to Max for finding it.

Some of Helen's stories are from *The Iliad* and *The Odyssey* by Homer; from the plays of Euripides; from *Faust* by Goethe; from *Helen in Egypt* by H.D.; from *The Goddesses of Chaldea, Syria and Egypt* by Lawrence Durdin-Robertson; and from *The Encyclopedia Brittanica, Thirteenth Edition*.

The story of Chin-nu is from *The Goddesses of India, Tibet, China and Japan* by Lawrence Durdin-Robertson.

The story of Oshun is from a discussion with Luisah Teish, thank you so much; and also from *Macumba: The Teachings of Maria-Jose, Mother of the Gods* by Serge Bramly.

The American Indian story of Yellow Woman is in Cochiti stories collected by Ruth Benedict; in BIA ethnographic collections; and from lengthy discussion with Paula Gunn Allen. Other versions appear in *Schat-Chen* by John M. Gunn. Leslie Marmon Silko has a modern version, "Yellow Woman," in a collection of her stories, *Storyteller*. Allen and Silko are both from the Laguna Pueblo tribe.

The Ainu story of Fire and of Grandmother Spider is from *Songs of Gods, Songs of Humans* by Donald L. Phillips.

Some of the Greek stories are from Bullfinch's *Age of Fable*.

Thanks to Hattie Gossett for her article, "billie lives! billie lives!" in *This Bridge Called My Back*, edited by Gloria Anzaldúa and Cherríe Moraga. Billie Holiday characteristically wore white gardenias in her hair.

The story of Sky Woman is from "The Woman Who Fell from the Sky, A Seneca Account" in *Literature of the American Indian*, edited by Thomas E. Sanders (Nippawanock-Cherokee) and Walter W. Peek (Metacomet-Narragansett-Wampanoag). It is also from "Creation Story, A Mohawk Account," in the *1982 Akwesasne Notes Calendar*. In the Mohawk version, Grandmother favored Flint over Sapling, and the male figure was sick rather than Sky Woman.

110

The Triangle Fire story is from a book of the same title; also from *Labor Heroines: Ten Women Who Led the Struggle* by Joyce Maupin. Rose Schneiderman was the organizer who made a speech in a whisper; one hundred forty-three young women died in the 1911 fire, trapped because the doors were locked to keep out organizers. Hannah, Angelina and Ellie are names of my conjecture; one of the women did throw out her hat and the contents of her purse in a grand gesture before leaping eight stories.

The oldest Sleeping Beauty story is from information given to me by Katharyn Machan Aal.